3

D1083606

SILENT CHASE

SUBMARINES OF THE U.S. NAVY

PHOTOGRAPHY BY STEVE AND YOGI KAUFMAN

FOREWORD BY TOM CLANCY

PAGE 1: *Deck, USS **Georgia** (SSBN 729).*
PAGES 2-3: *USS **George Washington Carver***
(SSBN 656), Holy Loch, Scotland.
PAGES 4-5: *USS **Guitarro** (SSN 665), left, and USS*
***Haddock** (SSN 621), San Diego, California.*
PAGE 6: *USS **Salt Lake City** (SSN 716).*
BELOW: *Line handlers, USS **Ohio** (SSBN 726).*
RIGHT: *USS **City of Corpus Christi** (SSN 705).*

Published by Thomasson-Grant, Inc.: Frank L. Thomasson III and
John F. Grant, Directors; C. Douglas Elliott, Product Development;
Mary Alice Parsons, Art Director; Carolyn M. Clark, Creative
Director; Hoke Perkins, Senior Editor; Jim Gibson, Production
Manager.
Designed by Mary Alice Parsons
Edited by Rebecca Beall Barns
Introduction and essays copyright © 1989 Yogi Kaufman.
Foreword copyright © 1989 Tom Clancy.
Copyright © 1989 by Thomasson-Grant, Inc. All rights reserved.
Photographs copyright © 1989 as credited on page 160. This
book, or any portions thereof, may not be reproduced in any form
without written permission of the publisher.
Color separations by Pioneer Graphic
through CGI (Malaysia) Sdn. Bhd.
Printed and bound in Japan by Dai Nippon Printing Co., Ltd.

Any inquiries should be directed to Thomasson-Grant, Inc., One
Morton Drive, Suite 500, Charlottesville, Virginia 22901, telephone
(804) 977-1780.

Library of Congress Cataloging-in-Publication Data

Kaufman, Steve.
    Silent chase.

    1. United States.   Navy—Submarine forces—
Pictorial works.   2. United States.   Navy—Submarine
forces.   3. Submarine boats—United States—
Pictorial works.   4. Submarine boats—United States.
I. Kaufman, Yogi.   II. Title.
V858.K38 1989   359.3'257'0973   88-40526
ISBN 0-934738-38-6

THOMASSON-GRANT

PAGES 10-11 AND ABOVE: *USS **San Francisco** (SSN 711). An attack sub moves out of Pearl Harbor for deployment in the Pacific. Each ship is given a number as well as a name. SS stands for submarine, SSN for nuclear attack submarine, SSBN for nuclear ballistic missile submarine; the number designates its chronology in the roster of submarines.*

They are hunters who live and work in an environment not meant for man. One might think of them as the first space travelers—or space warriors. Beginning in 1955, when USS *Nautilus* (SSN 571) deployed to sea, they were the first men to live in a completely enclosed environment, cut off from air and sun for months at a time.

Submariners make their own air, their own water, and their own light. Their only contact with the world outside the steel confines of their hull is through instruments, and those instruments are operated by a chosen few. For most of the men, the painted steel bulkheads of their work spaces are the world: 16 or more hours per day, seven days per week, until the boat surfaces again for the short ride back to port. Where the crew works below, a 20-foot vista is a distant horizon, and the sky is a pipe-cluttered overhead that punishes the tall.

The commanding officer lives in a "stateroom" that a federal judge would call cruel and unusual punishment if our country forced a felon to live there—not that he spends all that much time in it—and junior crew members are jammed into coffin-sized bunks that they must time-share with others. The crew's only recreation area is the mess room, where they may have time to see an occasional movie or perhaps a videotaped football game. For exercise, there might be a treadmill or stationary bike next to the "air machine" in the auxiliary room. All in all, the standards of accommodation would not have impressed the seamen who fought with John Paul Jones; they were at least allowed a drink with dinner—but the Navy did away with *that* around the time the grandfathers of these sailors were born. Factor out their pay over the hours worked, and it compares with what they earned in their high-school jobs, turning over hamburgers at McDonald's.

Why do they do it then? They do it for the same reason that a firefighter runs *into* a burning building instead of away from it like a sensible person. They do it for the same reason that a police officer runs *toward* the sound of gunfire. They do it for us.

*A submariner's family watches as USS **Michigan** (SSBN 727) goes through Hood Canal on its way to patrol.*

The sea, forbidding in its vast, featureless expanse, lured us long before we learned to write our thoughts. For at least five thousand years, there have been those who saw in the sea not a barrier, but a highway to distant places; not an obstacle, but a conveyance for trade; not an enemy, but a friend—albeit a friend of troublesome moods and uncertain loyalties. As luxuries and necessities began to move on the sea, people who wished to have those things—without, however, earning them by the usual means—found ways to make the sea a place of ambush and war. And so navies came about to protect trade, and thus to protect the nations that depended on trade. Well before the birth of Christ, it was recognized that national destinies could be determined by what took place far beyond sight of land. This principle was only haphazardly recognized until Mahan codified the theories in the late 19th century, about the time the first submarine was invented.

Attacks on trade began as piracy by individuals, then by organized bands and nations. Such attacks were formalized into a serious strategic plan by the French *Jeune Ecole* around the time of Mahan. Until World War I, the strategy of *guerre de course* was the work of cruisers—originally ships that sailed about on long missions—the pursuit of which became the work of other, larger ships designed for this purpose, called *battle* cruisers. When surface attacks on trade became too difficult and dangerous, a new kind of ship called a submarine—originally designed solely for attacks on warships—proved ideal for the task. In World War I, this new technology nearly decided the course of the conflict. In World War II it did, crippling Japan's national economy. After that war, won by countries that had both to defeat and apply the submarine threat, the message was clear: our fates would forever depend on submarines as part of a cohesive strategy for sea control, and the ideal weapon to counter one submarine was another.

The pursuit of reliable nuclear power for submarines had already begun in the 1930s—uranium used in the Manhattan Project was purchased by the Navy for these ends—and came to fruition with *Nautilus* (was it a coincidence that she was named for Captain Nemo's command?), and with U.S. Navy submarine number 571 began a new chapter in naval history. Soon the deadly hunter became the protector and partner of the fleet. Whether operating in close support of the battlegroup, or stalking the enemy at a great distance from his own quarry, the submarine's mission changed from sea denial to sea control.

The submarine hunts alone, in the dark. An enemy may reveal himself by the swish of his propellers or by the chatter of his hull responding to a change in water pressure. A contact may appear, then disappear, masked by spurious "biological" signals in the sea, by the rumble of ice floes, or by his own design. Success in battle is signaled by nothing more than a shudder through the hull, and death can arrive with a sudden flash and the enveloping rush of the sea, claiming the lives of the trespassers as surely as would the vacuum of space.

Why do the men on the submarines do it? Because theirs is the most difficult mission, the most arduous duty, the most demanding discipline, and these things have always drawn the best of men.

We can see the "platforms," as they are called, sitting on the surface. But as with all aspects of the profession, the secrets of the boat and her crew are hidden from casual view. We can count the boats, list the classes, and measure their dimensions, but their virtues, like those of the men who "drive" them, must be experienced—or imagined. When the submarines leave their berths, they dive and disappear for months.

For most, it is enough to know that the boats and their men exist for us. When an enemy submarine glides through the cold darkness with missiles aimed at America and our allies, one of our hunters is probably nearby. When another nation contemplates action at sea, it must give consideration to the boats that cannot be counted at their berths, and wonder about the location of the lonely hunters and the men who serve them.

—Tom Clancy

*A captain and lookouts stand on the bridge of USS **Ohio** (SSBN 726) as she returns to Bangor, Washington from a patrol in the Pacific.*

PAGES 16-17: *USS **Nautilus** (SSN 571), Golden Gate Bridge, San Francisco. When **Nautilus**, the world's first nuclear-powered submarine, sailed in 1955, it marked the beginning of an era: once submarines were no longer forced to surface or use snorkels to recharge batteries or replenish air, totally submerged patrols were limited only by provisions and human endurance. **Nautilus** went on permanent display in Groton, Connecticut in 1986.*

INTRODUCTION

Battlefields unlike any of wars past, the ocean depths provide an eerie backdrop for sleek, black ships. In the dark waters, submarines glide, alone and silent, some seeking enemies out, some avoiding them, depending upon their missions. The boats are marvels of technology, from their complex nuclear propulsion plants to their missiles, torpedoes, fire control systems, and sensors which can detect an enemy's noise signature or electronic signal.

Watch a submarine dive in the most transparent waters of this battleground. In only a few fathoms, the ocean swallows it up; its shape becomes less distinguishable as the rapidly darkening curtain of deep blue or green changes to the darkest of blacks. It is gone. The submariner's world is now controlled by sound and by the instruments which produce, measure, or detect it.

With the exception of some deep-diving research submersibles, submarines operate only in the shallowest "skin" of the oceans. In some distant war, subs with a more advanced capability may make use of the oceans' deep canyons, seamounts, and ridges. But today, the terrain of significance consists of thermal layers created by the heating of near-surface waters; currents and waves, which modify the movements of ships and produce noise; the ocean bottom and depth, which influence the propagation of sound; and sea life, which produces interfering noise and echoes—in short, anything that affects sonar.

The warriors are highly trained sailors, skilled in operating complex equipment and endowed with a heritage of success. All are important, for submarine operation is team play at its zenith, but on this battlefield the point men are the sonarmen who find the enemy, identify him, and provide the information necessary for attack or evasion. Listening intently and watching visual indications, sonarmen pull contacts from the background ocean noise, contacts which could be enemy subs. This deep and eerie battleground, at times so silent that an efficient sonar might detect noises made by a bad motor bearing miles distant, can at other times

Launch of USS **Will Rogers** *(SSBN 659), Groton, Connecticut, 1966. The Polaris submarines were the first to launch U.S. ballistic missiles from underwater platforms. Among those standing on the bridge of the 41st and last of the Polaris subs are the captain and his son, Yogi and Steve Kaufman, the photographers for this book.*

be a cacophony of whales squealing and bellowing, shrimp snapping, porpoises whistling, active sonars pinging, propellers thrashing, or all of these echoing from wakes and the bottom.

Here, the machines of war are vastly different from other naval ships. While the submarine's versatility makes it a valued ally to aircraft and surface ships in other forms of naval warfare, it is in submarine warfare that its unique qualities are best brought to bear. Fighting independently in the enemy's back yard or where he controls the air and the surface, attacking surface forces, land installations, supply lines, or a numerically superior enemy sub force—these are the elements of submarine warfare. A hornet's nest that other friendly forces cannot survive challenges the sub drivers of today, just as the seemingly invincible 10-fathom curve challenged the submariners of yesteryear to penetrate those shallow waters to attack land-hugging coastal shipping.

In this game of cat-and-mouse, the often narrow margin of victory goes to the proficient and the careful. A mistake—the clang of a dropped wrench, the swish of cavitation made by the propeller's accelerating too fast, the pop of a light bulb or capped vanilla bottle imploding as discharged trash sinks—can trigger an enemy torpedo. On these battlefields there are no rumbling tanks, roaring jets, blasting artillery. No band, bugle, fife, nor drum. Neither shouts of orders nor cheers of victory. On these battlefields, warriors whisper.

I consider myself a fortunate man. My 35 years as a naval officer gave me the happiest and most rewarding career I could have imagined, spanning every significant submarine development since World War II. All subs are assigned a hull number upon authorization; you can tell the vintage by noting its place in the sequence. The first boat I stepped aboard after graduation from the U.S. Naval Academy in 1945 was the USS *Permit,* hull number 178; the last I commanded was the 41st and last Polaris sub, USS *Will Rogers,* hull number 659. We are now into the 750s.

I decided that I wanted to be a naval officer at the age of 10. What was the driving force? Father a Navy man? Home near the water? None of the above, unless the muddy and polluted Anacostia River qualifies. The answer is three films starring Dick Powell, Ruby Keeler, Lionel Barrymore, and Jimmy Stewart: "Flirtation Walk," "Navy Blue and Gold," and "Shipmates Forever." Leaving a job as a plumber's laborer laying the sewers of the Pentagon in July 1942, I hitchhiked to Annapolis and learned the rudiments of naval command. Shortly before graduation in the spring of 1945, I heard a lecture by Slade Cutter, an eminent sub skipper, multiple Navy Cross winner, football hero, and boxing champion. His type of ship sounded like the most effective weapon in the war effort, and I wanted in.

USS **Barb** (SS 220) Pearl Harbor, Hawaii, circa 1944. Until the close of World War II, submarines traveled mostly on the surface for speed. **Barb**'s flared bow optimized her surface speed for long transits, enabling the sub to run for attack position ahead of slower convoys and merchant ships. Commanders could conserve torpedoes by using deck guns against undefended or damaged ships.

"In" became a short stint aboard *Permit* prior to entering the Submarine School in New London, Connecticut. The sub was impressive: 23 silhouettes of sunken enemy ships emblazoned her conning tower. My most significant contribution to her war effort was, as duty officer, granting the crew permission to blow the whistle in celebration of VJ night, and blow it they did, for hours! In my naiveté, I didn't realize that such expenditure of air and splendid noise would so lower the pressure in our compressed air banks that *Permit* was pier-bound the next day due to insufficient air to start the diesel engines. In the euphoria of victory, nobody really cared. As I've told my wife a number of times since, timing is *so* important. They don't want you if you're not lucky.

Several months later I reported aboard *Atule* (SS 403). Greeted by a confident skipper who sported a Navy Cross and other awards, I was warmed by the reception and the camaraderie of the officers who, save the captain, were all on a nickname basis. The crew and officers revered "Captain Jack" or "the Old Man," sobriquets not used within his earshot. When the captain asked me if I could handle the dive, I piped up, "Yes, sir!" Acting as diving officer meant overseeing the opening of main ballast tank vents, sealing up the sub, and ballasting and trimming the ship by pumping water back and forth or in and out until the sub could be controlled, at very slow speed at periscope depth, with minimal use of the diving control planes.

Having accomplished a decent trim, I announced in my most businesslike tone, "Final trim, 65 feet!" The formality signified that I could handle the ship without added speed and turned over speed control to the conning officer. The annunciator repeaters, which show the speed order given to the main motors, indicated "stop." I needed to fine-tune my trim. When the next order came, "back two-thirds," I was perplexed. I told the captain that you can't control while backing, and his response was, "Who says so?" I tried to reverse my thinking, treating the bow planes as stern planes, and vice versa, and soon we were wallowing on the surface. Finally, by blowing and venting the bow buoyancy tank, I managed to head *Atule* back under while reversing. The next few hours brought me casualty drills of every variety: flooding, collision, fire, blackout, loss of power to controlling planes, you name it. This was the beginning of "hell year." Plebe year at Annapolis had been a lark by comparison.

At the end of my watch, I went forward for a cup of coffee, certain that I had "flunked submarine." While I had no way of appreciating it then, I probably received more personal attention from the captain during my first watch than some of my contemporaries serving in larger surface ships would receive in their entire careers.

On my second day aboard *Atule,* I was assigned the job of electronics officer. Although radar was a new and mysterious gadget, I had

USS **Pickerel** (SS 524), Hawaii, 1952. Water rushing from her superstructure, the diesel-electric **Pickerel** surfaces at a 48 degree angle. The submarine was one in a series of GUPPY (Greater Underwater Propulsion Power) conversions which doubled battery capacity and added a snorkel, allowing engines to operate while submerged. Such submarines were capable of high-speed angles and fast turns.

*Control room, USS **Jacksonville** (SSN 699). When the sun goes down, the control room is "rigged for red" so that the crew has night vision in case the ship has to surface. The periscope can be rotated 360 degrees during observations, a maneuver some describe as "dancing with a one-eyed lady."*

been exposed to its principles for one or two weeks at Annapolis and at Sub School. As "George," the junior officer on board, I was to be the commissary officer as well. I was also to relieve the first lieutenant when he was transferred to shore duty. The last task, which I had to take on sooner than planned, was a real challenge, since it involved caring for the topside and fittings, tanks, and all auxiliary systems in the ship— hydraulics, air compressors, periscopes, control planes, steering, hatches and doors, ventilation, and the freshwater system. Some referred to this catchall job as "officer in charge of stinks and leaks." I had a lot on my inexperienced hands. Learning came fast and furious, not only in the submarine systems, but also in the handling of people.

What I did not know until some time after receiving my gold submarine dolphins a year later, was that "the Old Man" had a theory: load down the new officer, and he will grow to meet the challenge. In less than 12 months on board, I made numerous landings in the tricky currents of New London's Thames River, acted as diving officer daily, practiced attacks on targets, most from periscope depth, but some while slashing in at 20 knots toward a darkened destroyer or a group of surface ships, and shot torpedoes in actual firing runs. I had the unique experience of participating in a 1946 Arctic exploration, diving under the polar ice cap (and hitting it) without the benefit of the efficient equipment now available. Finally, as duty officer with only the duty section of some 20 men on board, I took the ship to sea as a hurricane hit port. We anchored, dived, and rode it out sitting on the bottom.

Where else in the Navy could a young officer have found the challenges and confidence-building experiences available in submarines? My contemporaries encountered the same type of indoctrination; some perhaps more, some less. In the postwar years, we grew rapidly, and we were promoted slowly, but we were hooked on submarines. We were the hard core, a group of officers commissioned over a decade, who helped move the diesel sub Navy into the realm of the atom and missile.

At a bar in Key West, Florida, where the crew of USS *Seawolf* (SSN 575), the Navy's newest and finest nuclear sub, hung out during visits, a chief petty officer—a veteran of World War II submarine patrols, depth charges, ship sinkings, and similar challenges which add up to experience—poked fun at *Seawolf*'s sailors, his former shipmates in the diesel sub Navy. As *Seawolf*'s executive officer, bedecked with my brand-new rank of lieutenant commander, I had been called on by our crew to square away the "old" chief (who was probably in his mid-30s).

After prolonged razzing back and forth, I invited him to ride the ship next day with other submariners for whom we were going through our paces. Some of the old hands were a bit wary of the prima donna aura surrounding nuclear subs. As one of only two operating nuclear subs in the new nuclear Navy, we were visited almost daily by dignitaries and received high visibility in the media and high priority in funding. I taunted him with the thought that he might really be a little—just a little—afraid to take large dive angles at *Seawolf*'s high speeds.

Seawolf, like her predecessor *Nautilus,* was a fantastic submarine. Not only were her ship control and engineering systems built to the most exacting specifications with unprecedented quality assurance, but her habitability far surpassed that of previous subs. Internal construction featured color-coordinated formica, vinyl floor coverings, increased crew bunk area, adequate personal lockers, and much improved air-conditioning capacity. Furthermore, unlike her diesel-powered forerunners, her steam propulsion plant permitted the luxury of plentiful fresh water. Many diesel sailors on completing a ride on an SSN, or attack nuclear submarine, returned to their ship exclaiming, "They even wash down their bilges with fresh water!"

On that day in 1957, the chief saw a submarine which could operate at a sustained high speed—for weeks or months if necessary—with no need to surface for air, charge batteries depleted from a day's operation, or, for that matter, even depend upon periscopes for attack information. The ship could glide effortlessly with up angles or down angles and level off precisely at a desired depth, even with relatively inexperienced young sailors operating the planes. Used to the older diesel subs, which were forced to maintain a level posture while handling the almost two-ton tin fish, he watched in awe as torpedoes were reloaded in perfect safety with hydraulic controls despite large angles and rolls

U.S. aircraft carrier photographed through the periscope of USS **Narwhal** (SSN 671) at the moment it fires an exercise torpedo. Submarines have a search periscope equipped with radar, sensors, and cameras, as well as a smaller attack periscope for greater stealth at closer range.

while the sub maneuvered at high speed. A complete reload of weapons required only a few minutes, rather than the 20 or more to which he was accustomed.

Comfort? The entire ship, even the engine room festooned with steam piping, was actually cool in the humid, sticky Key West summer. No sailors slipped on decks wet with sweat. Missing was the heavy odor of diesel fuel, fumes which normally permeated clothing and left what submariners' wives called "the smell of dollars" because their husbands received extra-hazardous duty pay—later to be called incentive pay—for service in the undersea Navy. The chief found he could move around without sucking in his stomach when he passed others in the passageways. He found room to sit in the chief's quarters and the mess hall, and he marveled at the space between bunks.

As he observed a number of evolutions, the veteran of hundreds of dives was amazed at the ease with which the complex sub operated. The evolution of diving or surfacing lacked the clanging furor of stopping or starting diesels, of shifting propulsion; in fact, the quiet was almost startling. Depth changes were quick and smooth. The pièce de résistance was a fire drill, complete with heavy smoke. Although the crew abandoned the control room, the ship proceeded on ordered course and speed, submerged at a depth of 200 feet, and remained there during the 20 minutes of the drill, controlled by the automatic depth control system. (We weren't as cavalier as this may sound; the most experienced chief auxiliaryman and I remained to handle any problems. Technology had improved, but we were not complete fools.)

At the end of the day, the chief encapsulated a full day at sea observing the miracles of a brand-new type of sub with the comment: "Sir, she's one helluva *Cadillac* submarine!"

He volunteered for the nuclear Navy the next day.

More than 30 years later, I have to echo the chief's summation as I marvel at the newest attack and missile boats—the "nukes" and "boomers." Each sub is an improvement over its predecessor in quality assurance and safety. There is a sharpened attention paid to total system design and to the impacts on the entire system of seemingly unrelated modifications or repairs. The jury-rig fix is relegated only to emergencies as submariners have become increasingly educated in the nuances of complex systems; a mistake can be much too costly.

The opportunity my son and I had to visit and photograph 85 units of the Atlantic and Pacific submarine forces must be without precedent, and certainly it provides an unusual perspective even for me, despite my intimate, daily involvement with submarine operations for more than 20 years. But that was more than 20 years ago! Although the new boats are sleek, quiet, and sparkling, I was most startled by

Change of command. Submariners, nicknamed the "dungaree Navy" for their work clothes, wear Navy whites for a change of command ceremony.
LEFT: *Launch of USS **Pasadena** (SSN 752), Groton. Tugs surround **Pasadena** moments after launch to bring her to the pier.*

the appearance and condition of boats approaching the 20- to 30-year mark. Touring and photographing my last command, *Will Rogers,* I could only wonder at the superb stewardship of those who came after us. These older ships are advertisements for quality in hulls and systems, but also for the people who operate, maintain, and train.

In submarines, it always comes down to the people. The submarine force has always attracted fine, bright volunteers, and the explosion of technology has brought demands for even more smart young men. As the nuclear sub and Polaris programs hit their peaks, the Navy found that it had to enlist no fewer than 13,000 people annually to sort out 2,000 who could meet the stringent requirements for the nuclear submarine Navy.

Nuclear power schools evolved to provide basic academic education, and reactor prototype plants at Atomic Energy Commission sites were used to give realistic training in nuclear plant operations and casualties. In similar fashion, the weapons and supporting systems have become increasingly intricate; a torpedoman today is a far cry from his counterpart in World War II. Missile technicians, electronics technicians, and fire control technicians all have heavier demands.

Whether a submariner is an officer or enlisted, the education, training, retraining, and long patrols exact a toll in hard, steady work and absence from home, often for months without communication with families. It's a tough and challenging course, but the results, the capabilities and accomplishments of submarines, provide satisfaction and rewards. Young submariners examining formulas for career success cannot help but be inspired by the accession to the top by the present Chairman of the Joint Chiefs of Staff and two successive Chiefs of Naval Operations, all career submariners. There have also been scores of three- and four-star admiral submariners over the past decade.

Looking at photos of World War II submarine crews coming into Pearl Harbor, brooms lashed to periscopes signaling "clean sweep," I have to smile at the informal uniforms, the casual posture, and the carefree expressions. Visualizing those young crews surfacing diesel boats alongside enemy ships, bombarding them with five-inch shells and machine guns, and then boarding with 45-calibre pistols and Tommy guns, I can see a link to the seamen of eras past. The early days of submarines was a time of swashbuckling skippers and sailors with a will to win. The same will exists unabated today. Our submarine officers and sailors are the brightest ever, as dedicated as any ever, and face the most formidable challenges ever. I, for one, have absolutely no doubt that they will measure up — always.

— *Vice Admiral R. Y. Kaufman, USN (Ret.)*

*USS **Sunfish** (SSN 649), Norfolk, Virginia. The sail of a submarine has a bridge for conning the ship on the surface and retractable periscopes and masts for radar, radio, and snorkel.*

*Rescue vessel USS **Sunbird** and USS **Skipjack** (SSN 585), New London, Connecticut. First in a class of submarines with a whale-shaped hull modeled after the experimental **Albacore**, **Skipjack** was extremely maneuverable and capable of high speeds. New hulls are longer and more cylindrical to incorporate sound isolation technology and angled torpedo tubes.*

PAGES 30-31: *USS* **Pollack** *(SSN 603) and USS* **Guardfish** *(SSN 612) at their tender, USS* **Dixon**, *San Diego, California. Each class of submarine takes its name and number from the first ship of that class. When USS* **Thresher,** *which once lent its name to a type of attack submarine, was lost with its crew in 1963, USS* **Permit** *became the lead ship.* **Pollack** *and* **Guardfish** *are Permit class subs.*

*USS **City of Corpus Christi** (SSN 705). The design for the newest class of attack submarine, the Los Angeles, is now 20 years old. The Navy has plans for a larger type named Seawolf, which will have room for more weapons, sensors, and sound isolation.*

At the top of the world, a crack like a rifle's shot rings out as the sail of an SSN breaks the polar ice cap; bundled sailors spill out under the midnight sun to explore the bleak, Arctic landscape. On Sardinia's rocky coast, an SSN leaves a tender, heading out to its diving point in the Mediterranean Sea and its patrol supporting the Sixth Fleet off Libya. A North Atlantic storm that churns the surface of the ocean to froth gently rolls the off-watch sleepers of a 637 class 200 feet below the surface, as its sonar watchstanders record a Soviet sub moving south to its own patrol area off the northeast coast of the United States.

In the placid Indian Ocean, a 688 class shadows a U.S. nuclear aircraft carrier, providing sonar warning of approaching submarine contacts. Yet another SSN hovers in the Caribbean's crystal waters, as special swimmer units practice a "lock out" from the sub, float inflatable boats to the surface, reconnoiter an island, and return to the sub, undetected by land forces. As a Tomahawk missile destroys a blockhouse on a test range on San Clemente Island, California, a captain looks through the periscope and announces to his crew, "Heavy smoke high above target."

Streamlined, silent, stealthy—attack subs are the sports cars of the fleet, with the speed and maneuverability to dart in for attack against the fastest surface warships, matching them turn for turn. With sophisticated sonars they seek out their most dangerous foe—enemy submarines—in the dense, concealing waters of the ocean. Unlike ballistic missile subs, which do their best to stay out of trouble, attack subs look for it.

Their primary mission is countering the larger and increasingly quiet Soviet submarine force. In a duel of stealth versus stealth, the players count their acoustic advantages, measure the noise they make versus the noise they can detect, and strive to maintain an edge over their opponents through a combination of technology, tactics, and weapons. At sea and in port, crews spend hours upon hours peaking sonars to attain just one more decibel of sensitivity. They are constantly on the lookout for an improperly stowed item that could make noise by rubbing against something or channel the sounds of a submarine's machinery to the hull. Sonarmen monitor their hydrophones and probes to detect any unnecessary vibrations. In every evolution of patrol, from dumping garbage to singing hymns at Sunday church services, quiet is key.

Older ships have run out of room to incorporate the newest advances in sonar equipment and silencing. The Navy's inventory includes only a handful of diesels and older SSNs, which are being decommissioned by the time they turn 30. This leaves three basic types: Permit, 594 class; Sturgeon, 637 class; and Los Angeles, 688 class. The biggest and most recent in a series of progressively larger SSNs, the whale-shaped Los Angeles class measures 360 feet long (goal post to goal post on a football field) and displaces 7,000 tons, more than three times the displacement of World War II fleet subs.

In an age of microminiaturization, it may seem surprising that SSNs have grown larger as their technology has evolved. The requirements to beat a similarly improving enemy have driven engineers to design increasingly complex and larger equipment. Today's submarines must do more; the enemy is there in greater numbers, harder to find, harder to destroy, harder to escape, and the additional equipment, weapons, and crew to counter these challenges require more room.

Sonar in decades past fit into a single cabinet manned by a single radioman as a collateral duty. It might detect a loud, thrashing target from five to ten miles, but could not detect what we now consider a noisy sub at any range short of collision. Today sonar occupies much more space, including a room with a watch section of four sonarmen, an equipment room, and a large-diameter sphere in the bow, filled with multiple transducers. The SSN can attack the quietest enemy submarines before being detected by them; noisy targets can be heard for over 100 miles.

All warships exist to destroy an enemy, and SSNs are lethal. Tomahawk missiles provide long-range attack on ships or land targets, and Harpoon missiles are deployed against ships. Antisubmarine missiles deliver torpedoes at long range. The ace, though, is the Mark 48 torpedo. The 55-knot weapon uses wire guidance from the SSN's fire control system to steer, matching the target's bearing despite zigzags and speed changes, until the torpedo gains contact on its own pinging or passive sensors and moves to attack. The 48 can operate against deep-diving subs and the highest-performance surface ships, searching, acquiring, attacking, and if it misses, reattacking—repeatedly. The Sea Lance missile with torpedo payload, now under development, will provide even more capability against subs at longer sonar ranges.

The SSN arsenal's variety can pose a dilemma for skippers and

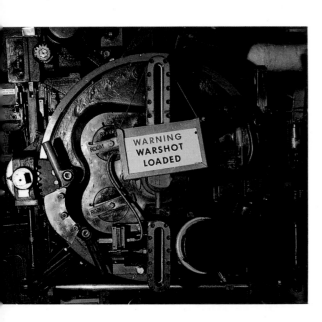

*Torpedo tube, USS **Andrew Jackson** (SSBN 619). A tag shows the status of a tube loaded with a Mark 48 torpedo.* RIGHT: *USS **City of Corpus Christi** (SSN 705). The bulge running the length of the hull of the Los Angeles class submarine contains a passive sonar system.*

weapons officers; with 20 weapons and only four loading tubes, it is difficult to prepare for all contingencies. The newest 688s are easing the problem by installing vertical Tomahawk launchers in bow ballast tanks. With increased weapons stowage and launching tubes, the proposed Seawolf, a class larger than the 688s, will do even more. Navy planners envision attack subs engaging in anti-air warfare, laying mines, carrying remotely piloted vehicles, delivering special warfare units, and launching surveillance satellites. In the eyes of many SSN drivers, the Seawolf class will clinch the acoustic advantage.

PAGES 36-37: *USS **Hyman G. Rickover** (SSN 709) and USS **Baton Rouge** (SSN 689), Norfolk. Hyman Rickover, a tireless and outspoken promoter of a nuclear Navy, was the man most responsible for its design and development.*

"Fast-attack submarines pursue enemy submarines, gather intelligence, support aircraft carriers, and deliver men for special maneuvers. Since we work in a demanding and inhospitable environment, we can't take anything for granted. If something on board doesn't sound, smell, or look the way it should, we assume it's dangerous until proven otherwise.

The long separations from family and friends are difficult for everyone. Extra pay will never replace that time, but we make the sacrifice regularly because it's so important. Submariners have grown out of a tradition that's different from any other in the military. We go places on our own and come back on our own; we have a lot of adventures we can't talk about. Even though our work is dangerous, we're not going to stand out as heroes. The submarine force attracts a different kind of sailor.

My biggest satisfaction comes from directing smart, capable people. Every submariner undergoes extensive screening, and most attend difficult schools to get here. All are volunteers. Even though I don't have the option of selecting my crew, I can be pretty sure I'll be assigned good men. Motivating them is my number one priority. If I can keep people fired up, not only about the technical aspects of their work but about the Navy itself, they'll do a good job, and they'll stay with submarines."

— *Captain*

Submarines, tenders, and destroyers, Norfolk. Some submariners joke that there are two kinds of ships: submarines and targets.
LEFT: Captain at periscope, USS **Jacksonville** (SSN 699). Leaving Norfolk on the way to a diving point off the continental shelf, the captain checks the passage of surface ships reported by his officer of the deck.

Officer of the deck and lookout, bridge, USS **Ray** *(SSN 653). When subs operate at periscope depth, they usually travel at three knots or less to avoid a telltale wake that would be visible to the naked eye, even at a distance. The fairings, camouflaged with spots, protect the periscopes and masts and reduce their wakes when the ship travels at greater speeds.*
LEFT: *USS* **Ray** *(SSN 653) and USS* **Sunfish** *(SSN 649), Charleston, South Carolina. Attack submarines undergo refit and routine maintenance at sub bases and tenders; major overhauls take place nearby at the naval shipyard.*

Submarines and tenders, Norfolk. Decades ago, when whole squadrons of much smaller submarines nestled up to their repair boats like nursing piglets, submarines were given the nickname "pigboats."

"You can't put a shipyard everywhere you have submarines. That's why we have tenders. With 50 different shops on board the tender, we can take care of repairs ranging from periscope alignments to hull welds. Our responsibility is to minimize, through excellent maintenance, the risks involved in submarines, and to keep the ships on schedule.

Any work we do on a sub's nuclear components has always involved thorough review. After *Thresher* went down with all hands in 1963, we created an additional program called SUBSAFE, which requires technicians and inspectors to sign off on step-by-step procedures that safeguard a submarine's critical systems. We document everything so that once a ship deploys, we can trace exactly what was done to it, all the way back to the origin of the parts and materials we used.

When we repair or make a new weld in a hull, for example, we use only metals that have met the strictest standards for strength and durability. Following a series of careful procedures, we inspect each layer of the weld for visible defects, then run a series of tests to check for cracks or weaknesses in the metal. One of the last steps is taking an x-ray to make sure there aren't any internal flaws.

The Navy doesn't build as many tenders as it used to. When money for defense is tight, we try to keep the older tenders running a little while longer. No matter how sophisticated new base facilities are, they're still stuck in one place. If we send a squadron of fast-attack submarines to a remote site, they'll need a tender to cut down on their transit time for repairs.

As it is, we don't go to sea very often, and a lot of submariners are envious that the tender crew can go home at night. But the people in my crew work 20-hour days if necessary, doing everything they can to relieve the submariners so they have as much time off as possible when they're in port."

—Repair officer

USS **Fulton**, New London. The 48-year-old tender provides mobile maintenance and repair facilities for subs at remote sites and at domestic bases. One mile up the Thames River, at the U.S. Naval Submarine Base in Groton, submariners traditionally begin their careers at Sub School. The base also has a medical research lab and mooring and maintenance facilities for two submarine squadrons.

FAR LEFT: Foundry, USS **Emory S. Land**. Metalworkers in a tender's foundry handle a variety of jobs, from repairing a hull weld to casting a new part for refit.

LEFT: Diver, USS **Fulton**. A diver checks out a decompression chamber for use in preventing the bends after extended underwater work at great depth. Divers can make some repairs to submarines at sea and in port, saving some trips to dry dock.

ABOVE AND RIGHT: *Loading supplies, USS* **San Francisco** *(SSN 711). When the only access to a submarine is through 26-inch and 30-inch hatches, loading provisions for a long patrol is a labor-intensive event for all hands. Repair work done by way of such small openings has been compared to building ships in a bottle.*
LEFT: *Loading provisions, USS* **Fulton***. Cooks typically stock at least a three months' supply, ordered through the tender, before leaving on patrol.*

Arc welder, USS **McKee**. Welding shops on tenders can custom-make, as well as repair, parts for submarines. RIGHT: USS **Billfish** (SSN 676), floating dry dock USS **Shippingport**. In driving rain, a crew blasts the hull of the **Billfish** with steam and sand to remove algae and other sea life that accumulate on the bottom of the ship and reduce her speed. When the ship docks for hull repair, it eases into a flooded enclosure. Then the water is pumped out until the hull comes to rest on wooden blocks. Floating dry docks can be towed where needed.

USS **Billfish** (SSN 676). After surfacing through ice near the North Pole, the bundled crew of USS **Billfish** comes out to inspect the ship for damage and explore their stark surroundings. The fairwater planes on the sails of some submarines rotate to the vertical position to avoid damage as the ship penetrates ice several feet thick. To surface, the sub finds thinner ice with special sonar. While the ship holds its position, the diving officer pumps the ballast out, and the submarine rises steadily and slowly to prevent damage to the sail or hull as they break through the ice. Operations under the ice greatly reduce or eliminate the effectiveness of anti-submarine aircraft and surface ships, turning antisubmarine warfare into duels between subs.

*Tender USS **Orion** and USS **Jack** (SSN 605), and (LEFT)*
*USS **Archerfish** (SSN 678), l a Maddalcna, Italy. A tender*
at La Maddalena, a NATO base off Sardinia, provides
supplies and maintenance for U.S. attack submarines
deployed to the Mediterranean.

*PAGES 54-55: USS **Salt Lake City** (SSN 716), floating*
*dry dock USS **Arco**, San Diego. Behind the glass-*
reinforced plastic bow dome of the Los Angeles class
submarine is a sphere of hydrophones, the main sonar
for the ship. The bow dome allows smooth water flow,
even at high speeds, preventing noisy turbulence that
might otherwise degrade the performance of the sensi-
tive sonar.

"On the boat, on the beach, and in the barracks, if a sailor gets into trouble, I'll be there. I probably know more secrets about the men on this submarine than any two chaplains ever have. I'm the liaison between the captain, his wardroom, and the crew. Since everyone comes to me, I can make a lot of difference by helping officers lead effectively and keep the respect of the crew. When a young officer asks a question, I give him an honest answer so he can make a decision. If it's the wrong one, we'll gracefully turn it around in the morning.

Often a man comes in confidence to tell me that someone's doing something wrong, but before I say or do anything about it, I have to take into account how it will affect our ship or our mission. Is it a problem I can take care of now, or is it one that I'll have to deal with later? Sometimes I get frustrated and raise my voice. Who knows how far to go? I've seen chiefs that a crew wouldn't even talk to because of leadership style.

A lot has changed in the past 10 years in the kinds of problems on board and the way a chief of the boat handles them. Ten years ago the COB's word was law, no questions asked. We didn't take time to listen to people, we just told them what to do.

Things have changed for a couple of reasons. Sailors have more education now, and their upbringing is different. Men raised in the '40s and '50s bought the work ethic, but sailors coming in today grew up in the '60s, a totally different era. They ask 'why' more than they ever did before. You have to gain their confidence before they'll do what you say."

— Chief of the boat (COB)

LEFT: *USS **Salt Lake City** (SSN 716) and Sea World blimp, San Diego. Line handlers secure **Salt Lake City** while the dock floods enough to lift the submarine off the wooden blocks on which it rested for repairs.*
UPPER: *Chief of the boat, USS **Salt Lake City** (SSN 716). The COB acts as liaison between the captain, his wardroom, and the crew.*
LOWER: *Cook, USS **Salt Lake City** (SSN 716). Cooks offer as much variety in their menus as possible, including ethnic meals and barbecues on the pier while the ship is in for maintenance.*

*Security watch, USS **Salt Lake City** (SSN 716). Anyone authorized to board a submarine or tender must present identification and state the purpose and destination of the visit before being checked off the ship's official access list.*
RIGHT: *USS **Salt Lake City** (SSN 716), San Diego. Engulfed in fog in a busy harbor, a submarine relies mainly on radar, fog signals, and skilled lookouts and officers on the bridge for navigation.*

Attack submarines and tenders, San Diego. The three most recent classes of attack submarines tie up for maintenance between operations. The 688 Los Angeles class, in the foreground, has a large, bulbous bow. The 637 Sturgeon class, moored outboard on the left, has a relatively large sail, and the 594 Permit class sub, moored ahead of it on the same pier, has a small sail.

*LEFT: Brown pelicans, USS **Portsmouth** (SSN 707). Numbers on the rudder indicate the depth in feet to the bottom of the hull, and the letters warn of a projection—the stern planes which control the angle of motion.*

USS **La Jolla** (SSN 701) under way, San Diego. The difficulties of mooring a single-propeller ship equipped with expensive and vulnerable sonars make tugs indispensable.

USS **Blueback** (SS 581) and tender USS **McKee**. Diesel subs must snorkel or surface periodically to recharge their batteries and replenish air. Since the establishment of the nuclear navy, diesels have been gradually phased out of the U.S. fleet. The remaining three help simulate enemy submarines in exercises.
UPPER RIGHT: Navigator and quartermaster, control room, USS **Blueback**. As a ship leaves port, the navigator and quartermaster work together to plot bearings and pilot the ship.
LOWER RIGHT: Auxiliaryman, control room, USS **Blueback**. One of an auxiliaryman's many tasks is to monitor and shift the submarine's ballast to compensate for any change in load. He is also in charge of a number of systems, including those for ventilation, waste disposal, drinking water, hydraulics, and refrigeration.

"With the exception of electrical systems and anything directly related to the propulsion plant, auxiliarymen are responsible for most of the equipment on board. By the time we finish repairs or maintenance on one thing, another system—hydraulics, waste disposal, drinking water, ventilation, ballast tanks, the diesel engines, refrigeration—needs attention.

We make our air from seawater that has been distilled. Using electrolysis, an oxygen generator breaks down the water into oxygen and hydrogen. We dispose of the hydrogen, vent some of the oxygen into the ship, and store the rest in tanks. When we're on ultraquiet alert, we turn the oxygen generator off and either bleed the tanks or use perchlorate candles, which release oxygen as they burn.

Once every hour we monitor a number of potentially hazardous substances that can build up on a submarine, including hydrogen from batteries, freon from refrigeration, gases from torpedoes, and carbon monoxide from tobacco smoke. Scrubbers and COH_2 [carbon monoxide/hydrogen] burners take care of most of the contaminants on the ship, including the buildup of carbon dioxide, which is scrubbed, compressed, then pumped overboard.

By circulating the air through charcoal filters, we can remove a lot of odors. Electrostatic precipitators collect cooking smells and cigarette smoke. Similar to the devices found in bars, the precipitators electrically charge smoke particles so that they collect on a set of metal plates. Since a lot of us smoke, particularly in high-stress situations, we have to clean the plates often. Even though the atmosphere on board meets high standards, we sometimes raise our snorkel to get fresh air.

We compact all our trash and pump it out of the ship in weighted cans so it sinks to the bottom. We're careful not to eject anything that traps air—one capped bottle could give us away when it implodes under pressure on its way down."

—Auxiliaryman

*Christmas in wardroom, USS **Blueback**. The wardroom serves as an officer's dining room, administrative work area, and lounge. The crew has a mess hall for the same functions.*

RIGHT: Christmas lights and attack submarines, Norfolk. So that most submariners can spend Christmas at home, a duty section of about 30 men, enough to get the ship under way if necessary, is stationed on the sub for the holiday. The men invite their families aboard for Christmas dinner.

LEFT AND ABOVE: *USS **La Jolla** (SSN 701) and tender USS **McKee**, San Diego. Signal flags, bunting, and dress uniforms mark a change of command ceremony for a submarine group commander.*

PAGES 70-71: *USS **Pintado** (SSN 672), San Diego. **Pintado** comes in at dawn to pick up an inspection team for an all-day Operational Reactor Safeguards Examination that includes drills and oral and written tests that measure the knowledge and performance of the nuclear-trained crew.*

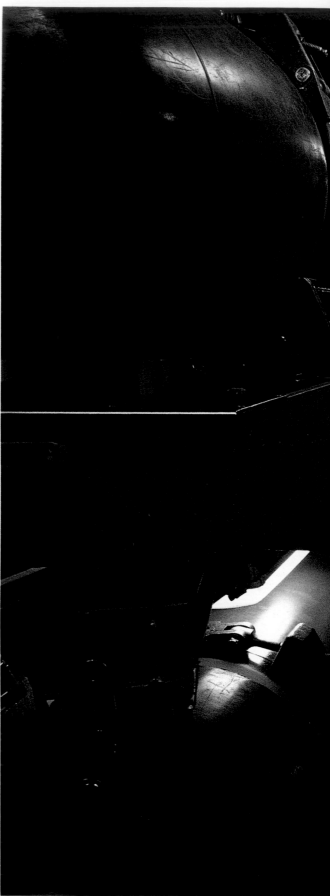

"When the captain announces, 'Snapshot 2, 1,' it means we've been fired upon by an enemy sub, and we're going to fire back in a hurry. Within 45 seconds I connect the torpedoes' communications with fire control, flood the tubes to equalize them with sea pressure, and open the muzzle doors. The fire control technicians in the attack center release the torpedoes.

The sonarmen are the first to know when a weapon shuts down or malfunctions. They track the noise the screw makes as it turns through the water; it sounds like a train. Low speed means the torpedo is searching for its target; high speed means it's going in for the kill.

The Mark 48 is a wire-guided, ship-to-ship weapon that explodes underneath its target, creating a huge air pocket capable of breaking the backs of even the largest ships. The Harpoon, a sub-to-surface weapon, penetrates the target's hull and, after a brief delay, goes inside and explodes."

—Torpedoman

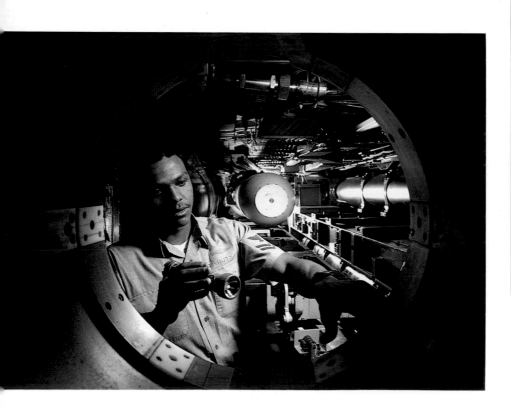

Torpedo room, USS **Omaha** (SSN 692). Mark 48 torpedoes are stowed on hydraulically operated racks that move the weapons into place for loading. After launch, the wire-guided Mark 48, capable of a speed of 55 knots, can be steered until it pinpoints a target with its own sonar. If it misses, it is programmed to reattack.
LEFT: Torpedoman, USS **Jacksonville** (SSN 699). A crewman inspects a torpedo tube before loading. A standard 21-inch diameter accommodates the Tomahawk, Harpoon, and antisubmarine missiles, as well as the Mark 48 torpedo.

*Loading torpedoes, USS **Key West** (SSN 722). After torpedoes are lowered into a Los Angeles class submarine by crane, they are guided through a hatch, tailfirst and at an angle, and placed on mobile storage racks in the torpedo room.*

"I share overall supervision of the ship with the captain so that he doesn't have to be awake 24 hours a day. As second in command, I carry out the captain's policies. To do my job well, I need to learn how he would react to situations. When he sleeps, I stand watch as command duty officer, giving permission for things the captain normally would, including coming to periscope depth and breaking rig for dive. I also decide when to use active sonar or send radio transmissions, actions that could give our position away.

As fire control coordinator in charge of the weapons systems during an attack, I take data from the sonar operators and the plotters to figure target solutions and decide when we've got enough information to fire. I've got to work quickly because there's always the threat that someone out there will be running the same scenario in reverse.

In old John Wayne movies, a guy at the periscope got a contact dead ahead, then gave the order to fire. It seemed as simple as that. In reality, attacks are much more complicated. A ship doesn't have to be moving very fast before it's out of the targeted area. You have to look at the angle on the bow of the target ship, figure its course and speed, then aim your torpedo to intercept it.

A submarine is a tougher target because with just sonar we can't get a sense of the contact's range. If sonar hears a submarine down a bearing line, we still have to solve a geometry problem to find out exactly where it is. The sub could be at any number of ranges and courses. Maneuvering our boat gives us more data for our fire control computers so they can come up with logical firing solutions.

Our biggest threat is another submarine. The technological gap between the powers is closing; our best defense against enemy subs will be tactics, training, and motivation. The crew that acts first and makes the fewest mistakes will win."

—Executive officer

*Fire control drill, USS **Salt Lake City** (SSN 716). The fire control team, coordinated by the executive officer, determines a target's range, course, and speed with the help of computers. The firing solution is then sent to a Mark 48 torpedo which, even after launch, remains connected to the system by a thin wire that plays out behind it until the torpedo's homing devices take over.*
LEFT: *Loading torpedoes, USS **Olympia** (SSN 717). In the Mark 48s used in exercises, explosive warheads have been replaced with buoyant caps that bring the costly weapons to the surface for recovery at the end of each run.*

UPPER FOUR AND RIGHT: *Tomahawk missile aimed at airplane in revetment. Launched from a submerged Los Angeles class submarine, a Tomahawk missile leaves the water and flies at low altitude to escape radar detection. Once over land, the missile follows a set flight path to the target, making adjustments in its course based on comparisons of its programmed flight path and the land below. The weapon is programmed to detonate above the airplane, destroying it in a violent explosion.*

LOWER TWO: *Tomahawk missile and blockhouse. Demonstrating an alternative method of attack against heavily fortified targets, the missile explodes on contact.*

UPPER AND ABOVE: *Divers, USS* **Cavalla** *(SSN 684). After leaving the escape compartment of* **Cavalla**, *SEALS (Sea, Air, Land Teams) open locker hatches on the deck to remove rubber boats for an exercise in special warfare operations.*

Attack submarine, Bahamas. Even in the clear waters of the Bahamas, the ocean quickly obscures a sub.

*Chief quartermaster, USS **Ray** (SSN 653). Although skilled in the use of a sextant, the quartermaster relies on NAVSAT, loran, and radar for precise fixes.*

"**B**efore we leave on patrol, I draw the track of our planned route on sea charts. Using information from the captain and the navigator, I lay down the course, making allowances for the ship's handling characteristics, currents, reefs, and other variables along the way. I keep a detailed log for permanent record that shows exactly where this ship has been on all its patrols.

There's a bit of artistry in the way I color the ship's tracks, and I take pleasure in that, but my work must also be neat, accurate, and easy to read. Not a minute goes by that I don't have to compute something. When the officer of the deck needs advice on where to turn the ship, I'm the one he asks.

We can use a number of systems to obtain precise data on our location. Loran [long-range navigation] gives us a fix based on radio signals from ground stations, and a navigational satellite called NAVSAT gives us another one. Fathometer checks tell us where we are in relation to the sea floor. SINS [Ship Inertial Navigational System] is a system of gyroscopes and accelerometers that measures the ship's speed, true course, and vertical motion with respect to the center of the earth. SINS indicates our latitude and longitude based on the ship's motion between external fixes."

—Quartermaster

If a submarine becomes disabled and cannot surface, the Navy has several means of rescue. A McCann rescue chamber like the one on board USS **Sunbird** (LEFT) was used in 1939 to save 33 crewmen of USS **Squalus** (SS 192) after she flooded during sea trials. The chamber can operate at a depth of 850 feet.

The submarine rescue vessel USS **Kittiwake** (RIGHT) places four anchored mooring buoys called ''spuds'' (ABOVE) around the distressed submarine. The rescue ship moves to the center of the four buoys and runs a seven-inch cable to each one, drawing itself directly over the submarine. The McCann chamber is then lowered into position over the escape hatch with guidance from either divers or a messenger buoy launched from the submarine. The chamber can transport eight to ten crewmen at a time.

Another means of escape is free ascent, in which submariners leave through the escape hatch wearing inflatable hoods that help buoy them rapidly to the surface. On the way up, the crewmen breathe oxygen through a special device in their hoods.

Submergence Rescue Vehicles (DSRVs) **Avalon** and **Mystic** are operated by a crew of four and can take 24 submariners on each trip.

The rescue vehicle can be transported by a C-141 (LEFT) to a catamaran rescue vessel (ASR) located on each coast, or by truck to a "mother" submarine, which carries it piggyback (ABOVE) to the location of the disabled ship. Once the "mother" sub has closed position, the DSRV is launched and finds the damaged submarine with the help of sonar, TV cameras, and strobe and flood lights. Thrusters help position the rescue vehicle directly over the escape hatch (RIGHT), clearly outlined in white. Once a connection is made, sea pressure holds the DSRV in place. At least five trips would be necessary to evacuate the entire crew of an attack submarine. Neither **Mystic** nor **Avalon** has ever been used in an emergency.

The Navy also operates two research vehicles for ocean exploration and the recovery of objects from the sea floor. **Turtle** has an operating depth of 10,000 feet, and **Sea Cliff**, with a hull of titanium, has an operating depth of 20,000 feet.

"Being able to tune in to one thing and tune out all the rest is what makes a sonarman a sonarman. When I went home for my first visit after sonar school, I was so programmed to count the turns of a propeller that I found myself counting the revolutions of my mother's washing machine several rooms away.

Everything in the ocean makes a unique sound, from sea leopards to submarines. We learn the propeller turncounts [the number of turns of the shaft per knot of speed] typical of different ships. A merchant is big and heavy, and its propeller turns slowly. A warship, built for speed, has one that moves fast. As the blades turn in the water, they cavitate, producing bubbles that collapse behind the propeller. The clue that gives a submarine away is the swishing sound of suppressed cavitation. Deep in the water, the noise is distinctive, but now there are oil tankers with such deep drafts that we have to get other clues to make a good identification.

In sonar school we listen to tapes and simulators and study the sound signatures of different ships on our video screens. The visual display cascades down the screen like a waterfall, giving us another way of checking our classification. Years ago before we had video, an interruption in the sonar room meant we'd miss something, but now we have a visual history of each contact.

Sometimes I can classify a ship by name as well as by type. Every vessel has a peculiarity that gives it a special sound—a unique piece of gear, a different propeller, an unusual engine. The Navy's rule of thumb is that 'until you see a ship, you can't be sure what it is,' so we continuously refine our classifications as we get new information. Sometimes we misidentify a contact, but it's always better to be conservative. I'll be embarrassed if I call something a submarine and it ends up being a fish, but at least we won't be in trouble."

—Sonarman

*Sonar room, USS **Atlanta** (SSN 712). Sonarmen classify their contacts by listening to them, monitoring their sound signatures on a video screen, and if necessary, analyzing computer print-outs. A sub's equipment and slight varia-tions in her construction can carry a sound signature so distinctive that sonarmen can identify some ships by name as well as class. Blue lighting enhances the cathode-ray tube displays.*

89

PAGES 90-91, LEFT, AND ABOVE: *USS **Honolulu** (SSN 718), Pearl Harbor. With a lei draped over her sail in a traditional Hawaiian welcome, **Honolulu** comes home after a six-month deployment.*

PAGES 94-95: *USS **Hawkbill** (SSN 666) and USS **Olympia** (SSN 717), Pearl Harbor. The anechoic rubber tiles visible on **Olympia** are designed to absorb sonar pulses directed at her hull. Submarine sonarmen usually listen for other ships with passive sonar that does not give them away; active sonar sends a pulse, or ping, that bounces off another ship, providing information on its distance as well as direction.*

This time the radio message ordering a missile launch drill comes shortly after midnight, as the smell of baking bread wafts from the galley. The control room is "rigged for red" so the captain and crew can see in the night should the ship have to surface or come to periscope depth.

The cadence of the SSBN's general alarm sounds, followed by the announcement, "Man Battle Stations Missile." Sailors awaken instantly, jump into blue coveralls, and hurry to stations throughout the ship. Operators give soft but crisp orders to energize torpedo fire control equipment should the launch draw an enemy. Sonarmen strain to detect the faintest indication of contacts as the noise made during countdown forces the SSBN from its black hole of silence. In the surrealistic red light, the now wide-awake crewmen perform check after hushed check on their sequence lists. Air whooshes through valves of the hovering system as the ship is brought to a stop. Other valves hiss as the pressure inside the missile tubes equalizes with sea pressure, preparing the large muzzle hatches for launch. The ship's exact position is verified, updated, and transferred to the missile fire control units as the countdown progresses.

In the missile control center, technicians monitor panels that light their faces like Christmas trees. With all systems go, the captain turns his key, and once the panels verify lineups and sequences, the weapons officer squeezes the firing relay. A gas generator ignites, propelling the missile out of the tube and toward the surface. A prolonged shudder rocks the boat, and the bow and stern whip up and down as a 40-ton missile accelerates, leaping into the air with a shower of spray. The ocean fills with noise as seawater rushes into the seven-foot diameter tube, and in seconds an automatic signal, sensing depth and pressure, triggers the hydraulically operated muzzle hatch to shut. The weight of the water permitted to enter equals that of the ejected missile, and the giant sub seems glued to its depth— only a temporary bounce of a foot or so registers on

*USS **Ohio** (SSBN 726), Strait of Juan de Fuca, Washington. The strait's deep waters permit missile submarines to dive near the pier, if necessary, and make their way undetected to their assigned patrol areas. Circles on the deck outline Trident missile hatches.*

ABOVE AND RIGHT: *Loading missiles, USS* **Tecumseh** *(SSBN 628), Charleston. Several missiles are removed during a ship's refit, enabling the crew to conduct casualty drills on the missile tubes during sea trials. After the trials, the tubes are reloaded for patrol.*

the depth gauges. Sonar operators hear the noises of doors, valves, and missile ejection. They raise eyebrows and purse lips; in an actual launch, this moment could draw fire from a nearby enemy.

Seconds after the missile breaks the surface, the first-stage motor ignites, lighting the dark ocean for miles as if it were day. With a roar of jets, the missile with its payload heads downrange where, this time, it will strike targets on a test range some 3,000 miles away in only 15 minutes.

Of all strategic weapons systems, the submarine stands alone in its survivability and, therefore, in its credibility. The first Polaris missile submarine carried 16 missiles, each capable of hitting a single target. However, because of the preponderance of bombers and ICBMs, the new weapons system did not gain prominence. Polaris later gave way to the more flexible Poseidon, which featured multiple warheads. Each of its 16 missiles could attack up to 14 discrete targets or saturate a defensive ABM system by aiming many weapons at a single target.

As strategic planners realized that weapons carried aboard submarines were less vulnerable than those in aircraft or silos, the 41-ship submarine force built between 1960 and 1967 rapidly gained favor. Today the SSBN force, including the most recent Trident submarines and missiles, provides approximately one-half of the U.S. strategic weapons for about one-quarter of the strategic budget and less than four percent of the total defense budget.

Trident submarines are built at a rate of one per year. At 18,700 tons, over twice the tonnage of older SSBNs, the 560-foot Trident is 5 feet longer than the Washington Monument and carries 24 instead of 16 missiles. Four full decks fit inside its 42-foot diameter hull, which provides space for quieting measures not available in smaller boats. When the larger, more powerful, and more accurate Trident D-5 missile is introduced, strategic planners will have a weapon capable of destroying fortified missile silos and command and control facilities.

SSBNs have proved reliable beyond even the Navy's expectations; more than 1,000 Polaris patrols were completed over 13 years before the first boat returned early because of equipment failure. A typical breakdown of the annual submarine budget shows more than 50 percent devoted to sustaining the force's high readiness. So that they can spend as much time as possible at sea, SSBNs are manned alternately by two crews, blue and gold, a measure taken at the start of the Polaris program in recognition of the submarine's limiting factor—people. Older SSBNs spend roughly 50 percent of their time making patrols of about 60 days, followed by crew turnover, a short refit period, and a brief tune-up at sea for the new crew before they go back on patrol. In contrast, Trident subs make longer patrols of 70 days, and over a lifetime will be at sea a planned 66 percent of the time, an even more remarkable figure for such a complex war machine.

Sailors on patrol constantly focus on noise control and sonar performance, because their highest priority, even above communications and launch readiness, is to remain undetected. The course of a ship on patrol is deliberately random. Top-secret operational centers know the huge area assigned to each submarine, but the only people who know the exact location of an SSBN are on board. Ship positions and movements vary hourly, according to distant contacts, sea conditions, the skipper's whim, and sometimes even the roll of dice.

Submariners often serve alternately in SSNs and SSBNs. Many prefer the more active pace of SSN operations, while others find the orderly and scheduled SSBN cycles easier on their family life. All would agree on the strategic importance of the SSBNs. As a commander of the Strategic Air Command once told his twins, both fighter pilots, "Boys, fighters are more fun. Bombers are more important!"

PAGES 100-101: *USS **Simon Lake**, Holy Loch, Scotland. USS **Proteus**, a submarine tender based at Holy Loch, established the first foreign refit site for Polaris missile submarines in 1960. It was modified to store 20 replacement missiles, a feature incorporated in newer tenders.*

ABOVE: *USS **Daniel Webster** (SSBN 626) in dry dock USS **Los Alamos**, Holy Loch. The floating dry dock and repair barges supply and maintain missile submarines.*

*Mailbags, tender USS **Simon Lake**, Holy Loch. Mail for an SSBN crew is delivered through her tender in port. Once an SSBN is deployed, the only way for relatives to communicate with crew members is through familygrams. Submarines receive regular summaries of news and sports, but communications are all one-way; messages going out could reveal the ship's location.*

"**H**aving a classified job gives us mystique. Since we can't talk about our work, people assume it's dangerous. I usually avoid mentioning my job when I meet people because I've come across so many who have no idea what it involves. It's easier to say I'm an electronics technician—the public can relate to that. There are always people who are violently opposed to nuclear power.

Deciding to specialize in reactors is like choosing a major in college, except that once we're here, we can't switch. It takes longer to train for this job than for any other on subs; after boot camp I had eight weeks of instruction in basic electronics, six months in advanced electronics, six in nuclear power, and six in a reactor prototype.

Our most important task is to maintain safe operation of the reactor plant, which provides the thermal power to produce steam for propelling the sub and generating its electricity. We're there to prevent things from going wrong and, in case they do, to correct the problem. The Navy has a perfect nuclear power record. We can't afford mistakes, so we train constantly. If anyone asks me a question about the reactor that I can't answer immediately, I know I need to train even harder.

Our radiation exposure is routinely checked and permanently recorded. Our readings are well within the safety limits, which are much more stringent than those imposed on civilians. On a three-month patrol I'll receive less radiation from the reactor plant than most people would from the sun. Our safety standards are so high and our exposures so low that my accumulated dose over the last 10 years is less than half of what a commercial plant operator is allowed in one year.

So much of what we do is misunderstood. When we say we're 'critical,' people think, 'The reactor's critical! It's going to melt down!' But the critical state is a reactor's normal state; that just means it's self-sustaining. In nuclear fission neutrons split atoms, in turn producing more neutrons. When you're critical, you make as many neutrons as you use."

—Reactor operator

ABOVE AND PAGES 106-107: USS **Will Rogers** (SSBN 659). After leaving Holy Loch, the Polaris missile submarine rounds the coast of Scotland.

If we ever have to launch our missiles, I'll be the one who actually pulls the trigger. When the time comes, I'll do what I've been trained to do, knowing that we've all somehow failed in our mission to deter. When the president gives the word to launch, the Joint Chiefs of Staff emergency actions team will encode a message and send it by radio to the strategic forces. On our boat, using independent sources from locked safes, a two-man team will break the code and present the message to the captain and the XO. After agreeing they have a valid order, they'll tell us we have permission to fire our missiles. The number of people needed to cooperate in a launch makes it impossible for one or even several unstable people to fire the missiles without authorization.

Any man considered crucial to missile launch is constantly evaluated in the ship's Personnel Reliability Program. If someone in the program has a problem, it's identified and resolved. Some people can handle stress better than others. If a man has a bad attitude, emotional troubles, or just not enough sleep, he's pulled away from nuclear weapons-related duties. We have a guard with a checklist of tasks each person is allowed to perform. Once a man's name is taken off the list, only the captain can reinstate him.

A number of situations can bring a man's fitness under review. If, for example, a guy gets a lot of parking tickets, it may be a reflection of his attitude toward authority. If a man has a drinking problem and can't take care of it with our help, he'll be pulled off submarines and nuclear commands and usually thrown out of the Navy altogether."

— Weapons officer

*Missile technician, USS **John C. Calhoun** (SSBN 630), Charleston. A technician checks the electrical connections to the explosive that will split a protective missile cover at launch.*
LEFT: *Missile, USS **Henry L. Stimson** (SSBN 655), Kings Bay, Georgia. Hours after return from a patrol in the Atlantic, the crew unloads a Trident C-4 missile. The blue plastic cover protects the missile from sea water from the time the hatch is opened to the instant of launch.*

Polaris launch control, USS **John C. Calhoun** (SSBN 630). The launch team goes through each step of launch in a "Battle Stations Missile" drill. Submariners stand 6-hour watches; in the intervening 12 hours they train, drill, maintain equipment, sleep, eat, and relax.

RIGHT: Missile compartment, USS **Michigan** (SSBN 727). The self-contained environment of each missile tube is constantly monitored to exacting specifications. Controlling humidity and ambient temperature is necessary to ensure the reliability of the missiles' solid propellant.

"I am responsible for a Trident launch system. I regulate the temperature and humidity inside the missile tubes, monitor the electrical power supply to each missile, and check the seal assemblies that allow a smooth launch. When we load the weapons into the boat, I make sure they're properly aligned. Floating cylinders inside each tube act as shock absorbers, protecting the 80,000-pound missiles from side-to-side motion in rough seas or in combat. It's a common misconception that an impact could cause a nuclear weapon to explode, but that won't happen unless it's gone through a very specific set of events that are part of a normal launch.

By the time you're a missile technician, the safety program is so ingrained that it seems you've been doing things this way since birth. Part of our program is the 'two-person concept,' which demands that two people always work together on nuclear weapons. We watch each other constantly to make sure no one violates safety rules and regulations, and use a rigid, step-by-step checklist.

We're a friendly group of guys. We have to be; we do a lot of our work in a very tight space. The compartment contains the missile's brains — the guidance systems, flight control computers, and units that activate the firing sequences. We have to stand right up against our partners, watching and verifying every move they make."

— Missile technician

*Fire control technician, USS **Daniel Webster** (SSBN 626). Fire control technicians verify the sequence of all computer operations during launch, assuring the smooth operation of computer guidance systems and the relay of coordinates for selected targets.*
RIGHT: *Poseidon missile launch, USS **Ulysses S. Grant** (SSBN 631), near Cape Canaveral, Florida. Before a submarine is sent on its first patrol and after each overhaul, it launches an exercise missile to confirm the readiness of its systems and crew.*

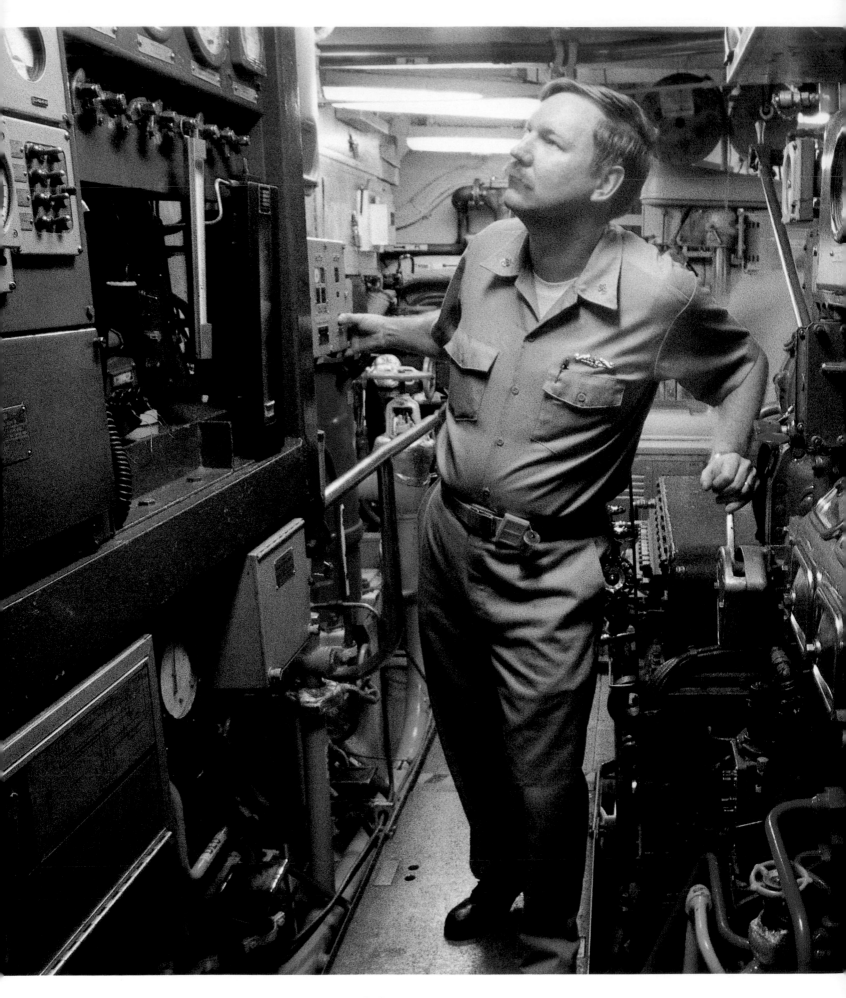

Auxiliary machinery room, USS **John C. Calhoun** (SSBN 630). Nuclear subs use their diesel engines and batteries for auxiliary power when their reactors are shut down. The yellow box on the crewman's belt is a thermoluminescent dosimeter which records radiation exposure.

Trident Training Facility, Bangor, Washington. Realistic drills prepare submariners for casualties at sea. At the Trident Training Facility, a pipe in an engineering compartment springs leaks, and as the room fills with water, the crew works to get the problem under control.

"The Navy wants executive officers to serve on both attack and missile subs so that we can become generalists. It's expected that one day we'll be commanding officers, and we'll need all the experience we can get.

There's a sort of good-natured rivalry between people on ballistic missile submarines [SSBNs] who evade enemy subs, and those on fast-attack submarines [SSNs] who pursue them. When I served on SSNs, we called SSBN crews 'truck drivers.'

The crew of an SSN can be sent off on short notice to do very esoteric things. It's an exciting and glamorous job. But from the standpoint of national security, the SSBN has the most important submarine mission: to keep a balance of mutual deterrence in a world of uneasy peace.

In my time as XO, I'm working out a philosophy of command for the day I'm assigned my own ship. A good captain inspires the loyalty, trust, and esprit de corps of his men. You've got to know your crew and let them get to know you, tell them what you expect of them, and then be fair."

—Executive officer

Emergency surfacing test, USS **Michigan** (SSBN 727), Dabob Bay, Washington. In an emergency drill USS **Michigan** surfaces after simulating severe damage and flooding. Compressed air was forced into its main ballast tanks at thousands of pounds of pressure to buoy the ship from a depth of 300 feet.

LEFT: Control room, USS **John C. Calhoun** (SSBN 630). One of the first assignments for an enlisted submariner is to take the helm or diving planes. Under the supervision of a diving officer, the crewmen pull their control wheels back to make the ship rise and push them forward to make the ship descend. Turning the wheel steers the ship to port or starboard.

Torpedo retriever, Bangor. A torpedo retriever has an open transom in the stern equipped with rollers to expedite hauling in torpedoes at the end of a practice run. The expensive weapons, used repeatedly in such drills, are fitted with nonexplosive heads.

Torpedo recovery team, Dabob Bay. Crew members secure a Mark 48 torpedo aboard the recovery ship. Although women cannot sail on submarines, many work in support services.

"From the maneuvering room, we run the reactor, steam, and electrical plants. The reactor operator controls the rods, the main cooling pumps, and the reactor's instrumentation. The throttleman monitors the steam and propulsion gauges and turns a large wheel to open the throttle valve, which releases steam to the turbines. The electrician regulates the distribution of electricity—at 2,000 kilowatts per generator, enough to serve a small city.

While these three do their jobs at the consoles, I stand right behind them, watching the main gauges to make sure we're safe. Sometimes it's easier to see problems when you've got the whole picture, but if I ever give an order that could have hazardous consequences, the men will tell me. You can't be passive on a submarine.

When the officer of the deck says, 'All ahead full,' bells ring in the maneuvering room, signaling us to open the throttles. Normally, the throttleman answers the bells at a specific rate to prevent the propeller from making a lot of noise, but if the captain gives us bells and then a buzz, it means he wants speed, and he doesn't care how much noise we make.

Casualties never happen just the way we drill for them, so we always try to add something new. One of the best drills is a reactor scram, or shutdown, because the minute you start it, it's no longer an exercise; an important piece of equipment could fail before we get the reactor up again. Combining a scram with a fire drill can make things really hectic, forcing us to think and improvise beyond established procedures."

—Engineering officer of the watch

Student, Nuclear Power School, Orlando, Florida. A student practices opening the throttle valve. Trainees work as many as 16 hours a day to qualify on nuclear plant prototypes before ever boarding a submarine. RIGHT: Students, Nuclear Power School, Orlando. As they examine the details of turbine blades and seals, students reinforce what they learn in intensive courses on turbine theory.

PAGES 122-123: USS **Nevada** (SSBN 733), Gaillard Cut, Panama Canal. A crew enjoys the topside barbecue that traditionally marks a submarine's passage through the canal.

LEFT: Threading her way past Panamanian pleasure boats, **Nevada** heads for the Pacific.

ABOVE: There are only two situations in which a captain is not responsible for the navigation of his ship: passage through the Panama Canal and entry or exit of a dry dock. "Mechanical mules" tow **Nevada** carefully through the lock gates.

US Navy Communications Station, Annapolis, Maryland. VLF (Very Low Frequency) radio waves transmit for thousands of miles. Because submarines can receive VLF signals with their antennas just below the ocean's surface, they can get messages without giving their positions away. An alternative communications system using ELF (Extremely Low Frequency) radio waves sends short, formatted messages to antennas hundreds of feet deep.

*Radio room, USS **John C. Calhoun** (SSBN 630). Radiomen constantly monitor teletype messages received over many different channels. They type and distribute any information of interest to the crew, including weather, news, sports, and familygrams.*

RIGHT: Sending a familygram, Bangor. Every SSBN crewmember is allowed to receive eight 50-word familygrams during each patrol.

"The radioman sends and receives all messages on the boat, from Super Bowl scores to orders from high command. On SSNs the signals usually come in through a satellite transceiver, then they're decoded by an onboard computer and printed in plain English on a teletype machine. When a sub taps into a constant broadcast, it remains difficult to detect, but an active transmission could give its position away. If there aren't any surface ships out there, it's easy to tell that the signal is coming from under water. SSNs only transmit when there's not much chance of being detected. In wartime the ship wouldn't usually risk it at all.

SSNs can get all the satellite transmissions they need by coming up to periscope depth for two minutes at regular intervals. SSBNs, on the other hand, must be able to receive at all times to be an effective deterrent, so they constantly use land-based VLF [Very Low Frequency], which can be picked up by a buoy under the surface or through an antenna that floats to the surface when the boat is at patrol depth. ELF [Extremely Low Frequency] can be received at great depth, but the transmission at that frequency is so slow that it's only used for short, formatted messages. If we don't hear it, that's an alert to come to a depth necessary to receive VLF or high-frequency signals.

When we're deployed for a long time, each man is allowed to get about eight 50-word familygrams. Sometimes we receive personal messages in codes that only the captain can break, so he can decide whether to tell a man of a death in the family and whether we can send him home.

Once a day radiomen post news and sports scores copied for us from the UPI and AP wire services. Sometimes it's exciting to get the news first, but it's not much fun when we take a message that says we're not going home as soon as we thought."

—Radioman

TACAMO aircraft, Naval Air Station, Patuxent, Maryland. Land-based communications centers which transmit radio signals to submarines are vulnerable to attack because they are stationary. The TACAMO (Take Charge and Move Out) system furnishes a mobile means of communication. TACAMO, a continuously airborne C-130 equipped with a radio relay station, is an important backup system for communication with missile submarines in case a launch order is given.

The aircraft has a five-mile-long trailing wire antenna which sends VLF signals. To transmit, the C-130 reels out the wire, flying in a tight circle to make the antenna hang as vertically as possible for submarine reception. The relatively slow C-130 is being replaced with the E-6A, which has greater speed, range, and protection against the electromagnetic pulse of nuclear blasts.

*Runner, missile compartment, USS **Michigan** (SSBN 727).
Nineteen laps around the missile compartment of a
Trident submarine equal one mile; a runner risks cut
knuckles and torn clothing if he takes too wide a turn.*

*Mess hall, USS **Olympia** (SSN 717). In their time off, crewmembers can watch any of hundreds of films on board. The mess hall is a center for meals, entertainment, training, and church services.*

"The crew has a lot of names for me—head cook, stew burner, the cookie. I serve 135 people a meal every six hours. If someone wants a sandwich or fruit in the middle of the night, he can have that, too, since I run a 24-hour restaurant.

The cook on board before me allowed music and movies during meals, but I don't. Traditionally mess decks have been sacred; on the old boats they served as both hospital and church. I hold with tradition—rowdy music shouldn't be played, and the men shouldn't wear hats.

Submariners feel closest to home when they hang around my kitchen. They read, study, watch movies, write letters, and play chess in the mess hall. When I'm baking, men sometimes come to the galley to talk and get away from the stress of their jobs.

Hamburgers are the favorite meal by far, but it wouldn't be healthy to serve 'sliders' more than three times a week. I like a varied menu, and I encourage my cooks to experiment. We follow standard instructions and recipes, but when it comes to sauces and spices, I let each cook come up with his own. I think it's more personal if the men can identify a certain kind of lasagna with their ship.

The Navy wants everyone to be trim. I keep the calorie count of my meals as low as I can, list calories for every course, and include a quotation on nutrition on every menu, but I never tell someone he shouldn't eat something because he's overweight. Look at me—I shouldn't talk.

The food on submarines is considered the best in the Navy. It's very important to morale. A menu review board representing different departments meets with me regularly to present requests and critiques. Sometimes I can tell whether the crew likes the food just by listening. If everyone talks a lot, it's a mediocre meal; if everyone really likes what's on his plate, it's very quiet. I also pay a lot of attention to what's thrown away."

—Cook

*Cook, USS **Narwhal** (SSN 671). Food on submarines is reputed to be the best in the military. Most of the baking is done at night, when there are fewer demands on the galley. RIGHT: Missile compartment, USS **Will Rogers** (SSBN 659). There is never enough room on a submarine. Cooks sometimes store fresh vegetables and fruits in net bags, in this case over a temporary bunk in the missile compartment.*

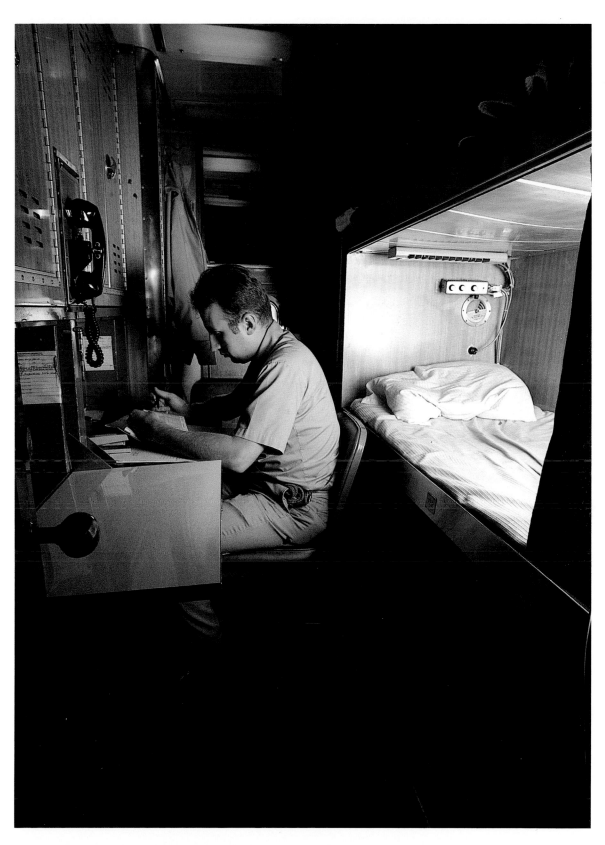

Officer's stateroom, USS **Andrew Jackson** (SSBN 619). Officers work and sleep
in their staterooms. In the captain's quarters, a panel indicates the ship's speed,
depth, and course; in many subs it also contains a TV monitor of the periscope's view.
LEFT: Bunkroom, USS **Portsmouth** (SSN 707). Bunks measure 18 by 76 inches
and have an overhead clearance of less than two feet, just enough room for a
man to roll over. On ships where there are more men than beds, some submariners
have to ''hot bunk,'' taking turns sleeping and standing watches.

Tender USS **McKee** and USS **Alaska** (SSBN 732), Seward, Alaska. Rigged in
full dress for the Fourth of July, San Diego based **McKee** services a Bangor
based Trident submarine.
LEFT: USS **Alaska** (SSBN 732), Resurrection Bay, Alaska. To dive, a submarine
crew opens the main ballast tank vents, allowing air to escape and water to rush
in from flood ports. Angled diving planes and speed drive the submarine down.
The rush of air escaping from the huge tanks makes a roar that can be heard on
the surface for more than a mile.

*Tender USS **McKee** and USS **Alaska** (SSBN 732), Seward, Alaska.*
RIGHT: *Engineering laboratory technician, USS **Michigan** (SSBN 727). The ELT regularly checks the radiation levels throughout the ship. On a three-month patrol, submariners receive less radiation from the reactor than most people do from exposure to the sun in the same amount of time.*

"Once a year the Navy's Nuclear Propulsion Examining Board reviews the safety of every nuclear ship in a two-day test at sea. It's the most difficult exam a submarine goes through, and so important that people keep themselves in training for it throughout the year.

The inspectors set up a series of simulated casualties and drills. They can shut down one of the turbine generators, for example, to see whether the crew can maintain electricity for the whole ship, or cause a reactor shutdown to see how skilled the crew is at getting the reactor back on line. They give every nuclear-trained man written and oral exams and inspect the condition of the equipment and the way it's stowed. The inspectors also review all radiation health records and how they are kept, making sure the technicians are proficient at reading the thermoluminescent dosimeters worn by each man to measure radiation exposure. In addition to the predictable Operational Reactor Safeguards Examination [ORSE], crews are given a number of surprise tests throughout the year.

If a submarine gets an unsatisfactory grade, it's taken into port and tied up until the crew is recertified. When I was an inspector, I could sense the crew's anticipation as I came aboard: 'Here comes the ORSE!' I felt like a black-hatted guy, but the exam is fair, and it's for the good of submariners and the Navy.

The Navy has an enviable nuclear safety record, and we can't afford to compromise that. Over the years as the ships meet a certain standard of excellence for safety, we continue to raise the standards. The exams are much more stringent than they were when I was a junior officer."

—Former nuclear safety inspector

The naval submarine base (RIGHT) at Bangor was established for the Trident missile and submarine, the third ballistic missile program following Polaris and Poseidon. The Trident C-4 missile has a range of about 4,000 nautical miles with a full payload and even more with fewer warheads, enabling Trident missile subs to patrol an area about 10 times larger than the Poseidon missile subs while maintaining comparable target coverage. A similar submarine base is under construction at Kings Bay, Georgia.

The Delta Refit Pier (RIGHT, foreground) can handle three Trident submarines, one on each side of the pier and one in the dry dock. The complex also includes a warehouse, repair shops, and offices for the squadron commander and crew.

The Explosive Handling Wharf (ABOVE AND RIGHT, background) is an all-weather shelter for loading and unloading Trident missiles. In a heavily guarded Strategic Weapons Facility elsewhere on the 7,000-acre base, missiles are assembled and stored until they are delivered to submarines.

ABOVE AND LEFT: *USS **Nevada** (SSBN 733), Bangor. Linehandlers secure the ropes that will, with the assistance of tugs, help ease **Nevada** into the Explosive Handling Wharf. Trident submarines are 560 feet long, five feet longer than the Washington Monument.*

ABOVE AND RIGHT: *USS **Nevada** (SSBN 733), Explosive Handling Wharf, Bangor. **Nevada**'s 24 missile hatches open, permitting final adjustments inside the tubes before Trident C-4 missiles are loaded for the submarine's first patrol.*

WARNING
RESTRICTED AREA
IT IS UNLAWFUL TO ENTER THIS AREA WITHOUT
PERMISSION OF THE INSTALLATION COMMANDER
(SEC. 21, INTERNAL SECURITY ACT OF 1950; 50 USC 797)
WHILE ON THIS INSTALLATION ALL PERSONNEL AND THE PROPERTY
UNDER THEIR CONTROL ARE SUBJECT TO SEARCH
USE OF DEADLY FORCE AUTHORIZED
325

Marine guard, Strategic Weapons Facility, Bangor. More than 300 Marines serve as a security force for the Strategic Weapons Facility, where Trident missiles and their components are stored in bunkers until their transfer to submarines.
RIGHT: *Missile loading, USS* ***Nevada*** *(SSBN 733), Explosive Handling Wharf, Bangor. Inside an all-weather shelter, a huge crane moves canisters containing Trident C-4 missiles into position over the tubes.*

All SSNs and pre-Trident SSBNs have 26- or 30-inch diameter hatches that make loading provisions for a 90-day patrol a large task. An entire crew must work at least one full day, passing everything down from hand to hand. The six-foot hatches and new container system of a Trident submarine allow several men to do the same job in about three hours.

The Trident's hatches make the removal and delivery of parts more efficient, an important consideration on a ship that carries more than 30,000 different types of parts. They also eliminate the need to cut open the pressure hull to remove large components for maintenance or exchange. Smaller hatches and trunks are included within the larger section for regular use.

For the loading of parts and provisions, the large hatch and trunk (LEFT) are lifted, and a box unit is installed to accommodate metal food containers (RIGHT), which slide on tracks into storerooms. Instruction manuals (ABOVE) are updated after every patrol so that each time a submarine goes out, the most current information goes with it.

Nuclear engineering petty officer leaving reactor compartment, USS **Michigan** (SSBN 727). For protection in a casualty drill that involves a major steam leak, an engineer wears a metallic, heat-reflecting suit. The umbilical cord provides a steady source of insulating air between his suit and his body.

USS **Ohio** (SSBN 726), Magnetic Silencing Facility, Bangor. In a process called degaussing, charged electrical coils minimize the magnetic signature picked up by submarines during construction and routine operation that could make them more vulnerable to mines and detection by submarine-hunting aircraft.

There are as many ways to lead as there are captains. You can try to do everything yourself, or you can rely heavily on your officers. My executive officer runs the ship from day to day, meeting with department heads and the rest of the crew to make sure that our schedules work and that the submarine runs efficiently.

I take responsibility for developing a crew so well trained that they will always work as a team, even under the stress of battle. Everyone specializes, but each man must also go through a year of general qualification on the sub. The cook, for example, knows something about radio communications. He also knows how to fight fires and where to find the damage control equipment.

We spend most of our time training, both in port and at sea, to make sure everyone is competent and able to perform. I walk through the ship a few times each day, finding each department's weaknesses and deciding how to turn them around.

Most of our attention focuses on being very, very quiet. When our sonarmen report contacts, we're particularly careful not to make any unnecessary noise. We must also maintain our lines of communication so that, if needed, we'll be ready to launch our missiles."

—Captain

USS **Georgia** (SSBN 729). A floating bridge across the Hood Canal opens for submarines in transit to and from patrol.
LEFT: Captain, pilot, and officer, the bridge, USS **Ohio** (SSBN 726), Strait of Juan de Fuca. As it enters home port, the ballistic missile submarine surfaces for the first time in 70 days.

PAGES 156-157: Sail, USS **Will Rogers** (SSBN 659). During surface operations the plexiglass windows in the submarine's sail provide views for the quartermaster, who makes detailed entries in the ship's log for every watch in port or at sea. The round opening is a whistle.

*Deactivation of USS **Scamp** (SSN 588), Bangor. One by one in dress whites, the crew of **Scamp** leave for the last time. Submarines are decommissioned by the time they turn 30 years old.*
LEFT: *USS **Omaha** (SSN 692), Hood Canal. Coming in with the help of a tug, USS **Omaha** passes heavily armed Marines stationed for the loading of missiles onto the submarine in the foreground.*

ACKNOWLEDGMENTS

The few words of thanks offered here can only begin to express our appreciation for the patience, understanding, cooperation, and infectious enthusiasm of the men and women—uniformed and civilian—of the U.S. Navy and the Submarine Forces in particular. We are greatly in their debt.

We wish to express lasting gratitude to the Chief of Naval Operations, Admiral Carl Trost, for his encouragement and assistance in setting the tone and scope of our efforts; to the Director of Nuclear Propulsion, Admiral Kin McKee, and the Assistant Chief of Naval Operations for Undersea Warfare, Vice Admiral Bruce DeMars, for assistance and helpful suggestions; to the Chief of Information, Rear Admiral Jimmie Finkelstein, for arranging our visits to commands near and far; and to the Commanders of the Submarine Forces, Vice Admiral Dan Cooper and Rear Admiral Guy Reynolds, for providing access to ships and personnel for photography and interviews.

Special thanks to Lieutenant Commanders Drew Malcomb, Tom Cole, Greg Hartung, Cathy Woodcock, and Sheri Beatty, to Lieutenants Joy Hopkins and Rob Raines, and to Chief Photographer's Mate Danilo Gan for coordinating our coverage and providing security guidance.

We can't say enough for the people on the subs, tenders, bases, rescue vessels, retrievers, tugs, floating dry docks, and in the schools. You were great! As usual!

—Yogi and Steve Kaufman

PHOTO CREDITS

Yogi Kaufman: Front cover, pages 1, 4-5, 8, 10-11, 14, 15, 26-27, 28-29, 30-31, 36-37, 38 (left), 40, 42-43, 44 (lower), 45 (lower), 46, 47 (lower), 48-49, 52-53, 53 (right), 54-55, 56, 57 (upper), 57 (lower), 58, 62-63, 64, 66 (left), 66-67, 68, 70-71, 72-73, 74-75, 77, 82-83, 84 (left), 84 (right), 85, 87 (upper), 87 (lower), 90-91, 93, 94-95, 96-97, 102-103, 103 (right), 106-107, 108, 109, 110, 114-115, 118-119, 119 (right), 120, 121, 125, 126-127, 128-129, 130-131, 132-133, 136, 137, 142, 150, 151 (upper), 151 (lower), 154, 156-157, 158, 159, and 160. **Steve Kaufman**: Back cover, pages 2-3, 6, 9, 12-13, 22, 24, 25, 32-33, 34, 35, 38-39, 41, 44-45, 47 (upper), 48 (left), 59, 60, 61, 65 (upper), 65 (lower), 69, 72 (left), 76, 88-89, 92, 98, 99, 100-101, 104-105, 111, 112, 113, 115 (right), 116 (left), 116-117, 122-123, 124, 129 (right), 132 (left), 134, 135, 138, 139, 140-141, 141 (right), 143, 144, 145, 146, 147, 148, 149, 152 (left), and 155. **U.S. Navy photos**: Pages 16-17, John Kristoffersen; pages 20, 21, and 23, photographer unknown; pages 50-51, Chuck Mussi; pages 78 (all), and 79, Naval Ocean Systems Command; pages 80 (upper and lower), and 80-81, Bernie Campoli; page 86, Lt. Cecil Davis; pages 152-153, Jan Sakamoto. **General Dynamics**: Pages 18-19, Electric Boat. *Lighting consultant: William K. Geiger.*